Contents

Flight 103's Last Moments 4

The Explosion 6

Lockerbie in Flames 8

The Investigation 10

Body Identification 12

The Bomb 14

The Evidence 16

The Trail Leads to Malta 18

The Suspects 20

The Plan 22

The Trial 24

Case Closed 26

Forensic Database 28

Glossary 31

Index 32

Flight 103's Last Moments

Pan Am Flight 103 took off from Heathrow Airport at 6.25pm, on Wednesday 21st December 1988. It was bound for JFK Airport in New York. The passengers and crew would never reach their destination.

Air traffic control tower at Heathrow Airport, London, UK.

Alan Topp, an **air traffic controller** at Prestwick Airport, Scotland, heard the final words from the flight. "Clipper 103 requesting oceanic clearance..." Another air traffic controller thought he heard a faint sound on the radio soon after.

Alan Topp watched a cross move across his **radar** screen. This cross showed the location of Flight 103, and how high it was flying. At 7.02pm, the cross suddenly disappeared from the screen.

Alan Topp tried to contact the plane, but there was no response. There were now several objects showing on the radar screen where Flight 103 had been. They were moving quickly apart. He had seen the plane explode!

> *Alan Topp had seen the plane explode!*

Radar screens display the positions of planes in flight.

An air traffic controller watches his computer screens.

The Explosion

The plane exploded over south-west Scotland. Onboard the flight were a crew of 16, and 243 passengers from around the world – 189 of them were American. All the passengers and crew members were killed.

The plane had been flying at 31,000 feet (9,449 metres). At that height, it took the **wreckage** more than a minute to crash down to Earth.

Most of the plane's **debris** fell on the Scottish town of Lockerbie. Some parts left craters in the nearby fields. Smaller pieces of wreckage were spread over 2,188 square kilometres of land. Some parts of the plane were carried 72 kilometres away by a strong wind.

The wreckage of the cockpit of Flight 103.

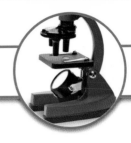

TRUE LIFE CRIME TRUE LIFE

> *It took the wreckage more than a minute to crash down to Earth.*

One of the engines from the plane crashed into a street in Lockerbie's town centre.

FORENSIC FACTFILE

The Flight

Plane:
Boeing 747–121

Airline:
Pan Am
(Pan American World Airways)

Number of Engines:
Four

Wingspan:
59.6 metres

Maximum speed:
1,024 kilometres per hour

Pilot:
Captain James MacQuarrie

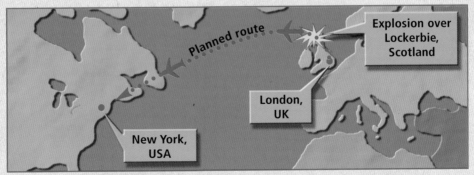

The planned route of Flight 103 from London to New York.

Lockerbie in Flames

A house on fire in Lockerbie after the plane crash.

The explosion rocked the town of Lockerbie below. Many homes were damaged by the falling debris. Large pieces of the aircraft buried themselves in the streets and houses.

When the wreckage of the plane crashed down on Lockerbie, 11 people in the town were killed. The wings of the plane smashed into Sherwood Crescent. The fuel inside the wings caught fire and created a huge fireball. Five houses were completely destroyed by the blast. In their place was a trench 47 metres long and 10 metres deep.

The area around Sherwood Crescent after the air crash.

Lockerbie looked like a war zone. Fires burned throughout the town. There were piles of crumpled steel everywhere.

> *The fuel inside the wings caught fire and created a huge fireball.*

Was the plane crash a tragic accident or had the explosion been caused by a bomb? The local police began an investigation with the **FBI** (Federal Bureau of Investigation) to find out what happened to Flight 103.

FORENSIC FACTFILE

How the Plane Fell Apart

- An explosion made the **front cone** and **cockpit** tear from the plane.

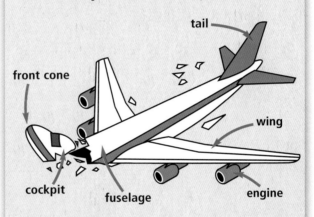

- The front section of the plane crashed in a field five kilometres from Lockerbie.

- The **fuselage** and wings of the plane travelled 21 kilometres further before they hit the ground. As they fell, they broke into smaller pieces. Most of the debris fell over Lockerbie.

- One section which crashed into Lockerbie contained both wings of the plane.

The Investigation

At first, news reports said that the plane had crashed into a petrol station in the centre of Lockerbie. People thought that it had exploded on the ground, not in the sky. Details were unclear, and most people thought the crash had been an accident.

In the months after the crash, more than 2,000 people searched Lockerbie and the surrounding countryside for debris from the plane. Police officers were joined by members of the British army and the FBI. The searchers worked in groups of eight or ten.

"Searchers were told: if it isn't growing and it isn't a rock, pick it up."

Investigators searched more than 2,000 square kilometres for clues.

Investigators carefully examined each piece of evidence found in the search.

The searchers tagged each piece of wreckage, and noted its location. Then each piece was moved to the gymnasium of a local school. Experts there used various scans and chemical tests to look for traces of **explosive residue.**

FORENSIC FACTFILE

Straight Line Searching

Police often use straight line searching to find evidence.

- The wreckage from the Lockerbie crash was spread over a very large area.

- The investigators hunted for clues using a technique called 'straight line searching'.

- In straight line searching, investigators walk shoulder to shoulder. They look up and down and from side to side.

- The searchers at Lockerbie were given a simple instruction: "If it isn't growing and it isn't a rock, pick it up."

Investigators walk in parallel lines so that every centimetre of ground is covered.

Body Identification

Investigators had to identify the victims so that they could understand how the crash had happened. They needed to know the names of the passengers, crew members, and those hit by the wreckage.

For some victims, this was difficult because their faces were damaged. **Forensic dentists** were called in to help. They could identify victims through their **dental records**.

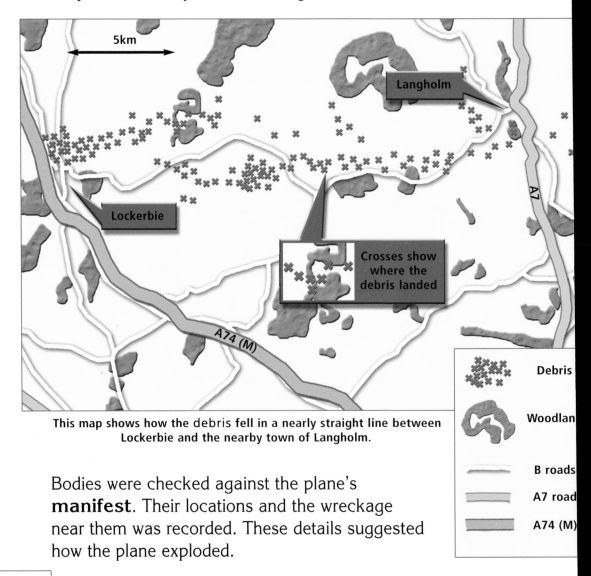

This map shows how the debris fell in a nearly straight line between Lockerbie and the nearby town of Langholm.

Bodies were checked against the plane's **manifest**. Their locations and the wreckage near them was recorded. These details suggested how the plane exploded.

FORENSIC FACTFILE

Forensic Dentists

- Forensic dentists help identify people. They may have to do this when the victim cannot be recognised because of facial injury.

- They note the shape and position of the teeth of a dead body. Do the teeth have fillings, caps or braces? Such items are compared to old x-rays or reports.

- If there are no dental records, photographs are used. The teeth and jaws in the photos are compared to the victims'.

- Forensic dentists can sometimes identify a person from a single tooth.

The only way to identify a skull like this one is through dental records.

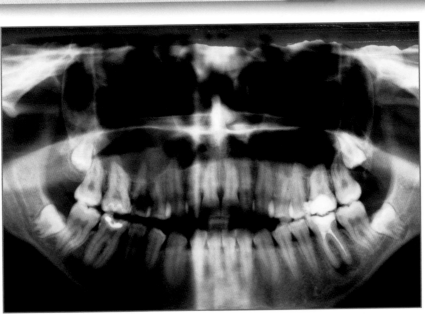

Each person's teeth are unique. Forensic dentists compare x-rays of corpses' teeth to records from dentists' surgeries.

The Bomb

Five days after the crash, investigators were still looking through the twisted metal. They found pieces of a suitcase and cassette player. Could they have been part of a bomb? The pieces of debris were sent to bomb experts.

Fragments of a Toshiba cassette
player were found in the wreckage.

On 26th December 1988, a week after the crash, bomb experts confirmed that they had found traces of explosive residue. They knew that someone had put a bomb on the plane, and murdered 270 innocent people. That is how the plane crash became a criminal investigation.

A bomb made from **plastic explosives** was hidden inside a Toshiba cassette player. The cassette player was wrapped in clothing. Someone had then placed these items inside a hard suitcase with an umbrella. Once the suitcase was on board, Flight 103 was doomed.

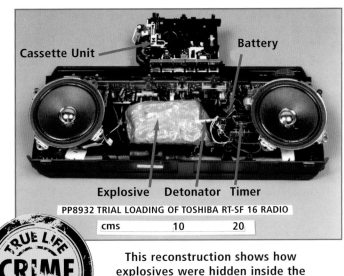

Cassette Unit

Battery

Explosive   Detonator Timer

PP8932 TRIAL LOADING OF TOSHIBA RT-SF 16 RADIO

cms   10   20

This reconstruction shows how explosives were hidden inside the cassette player.

FORENSIC FACTFILE

Explosives

Dynamite is a high explosive.

There are two types of explosives.

- **Low explosives:** These explode by burning very quickly. They are usually started by a flame. They are not as dangerous as high explosives.

- **High explosives:** These explode more violently than low explosives. They are used in weapons and demolition. Some high explosives are very **unstable**, and may explode without warning if not handled correctly. Flight 103 was destroyed by high explosives.

The Evidence

Investigators looked through 4 million pieces of wreckage. Every piece was taken to a **hangar** at Longtown, in Cumbria. There, workers put the plane together like a jigsaw puzzle.

When the main part of the fuselage neared completion, investigators saw a hole in the **cargo hold** 50 centimetres wide. A bomb had clearly made the hole. Metal panels on the outside of the hole were folded back and this was why the plane had come apart as it fell.

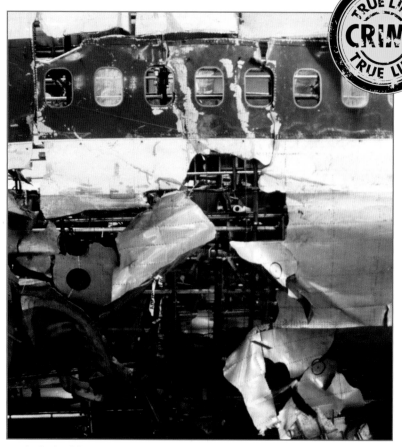

A hole had been torn in the fuselage on the left side of the plane.

"Workers put the plane together like a jigsaw puzzle."

FORENSIC FACTFILE

Semtex

The bomb was made of a powerful plastic explosive called Semtex. Other materials were used, too.

Semtex is sold in solid blocks.

- Adding plastic to an explosive makes it less likely to explode unexpectedly. This means that the bomb is easier to manage.

- Plastic explosives are soft, and can be shaped by hand.

- X-ray machines in airports cannot detect Semtex. However it can sometimes be discovered by **sniffer dogs**.

TRUE LIFE CRIME TRUE LIFE

The fragments of the bomb, the suitcase and the cassette player were special items. Bomb experts in the UK and America studied them closely.

They hoped that with this evidence they would find who had made the bomb.

The skin of the fuselage had folded open in a 'starburst' shape. This was evidence of an explosion.

The Trail Leads to Malta

World Map
(inset: Sliema, Malta)

The scraps of clothes found with the bomb had labels that said 'Yorkie', and 'Made in Malta'. These were important clues.

Investigators found out which shops in Malta sold Yorkie clothing. This led them to a shop called 'Mary's House', in Sliema, Malta. Its owner, Tony Gauci, gave the police an exact description of a customer who bought the clothes with the labels. This customer became the prime suspect. Police kept the store under **surveillance** in case he showed up again. However, they soon discovered that he had fled the country.

An artist's impression (left) and **photofit** (right) of the man who bought the clothes wrapped around the bomb. These were based on the description given to the police by Tony Gauci.

'Mary's House', the shop where some of the items found with the bomb were bought.

FORENSIC FACTFILE

The Clothes Evidence

The suspect bought a number of items at Mary's House in Malta. The items included:

- A grey shirt
- A cardigan with a tag marked 'Mary's House'
- A blue sleepsuit for a baby

When the suspect went to leave, it began to rain. The owner, Tony Gauci, convinced him to buy an umbrella.

The umbrella and other items were found in the wreckage of the plane. They were all covered with explosive material.

This clothes label from the grey shirt led the police to Malta.

A black umbrella was packed with the bomb.

The Suspects

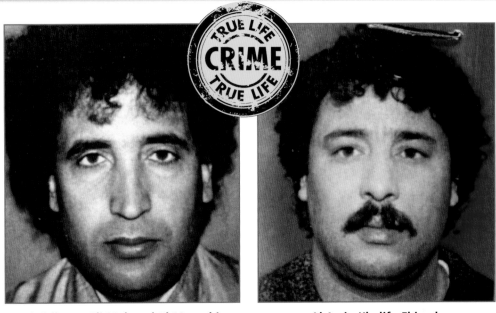

Abdelbaset Ali Mohmed Al Megrahi

Al Amin Khalifa Fhimah

The evidence gathered by the British police and the FBI led them to suspect two men of causing the Lockerbie disaster.

Pieces of a **timing device** for a bomb were found in the wreckage of Flight 103. They were linked to Abdelbaset Ali Mohmed Al Megrahi. He was an officer in the Libyan government and head of security at Libyan Arab Airlines. He was also identified as having bought clothes from the shop Mary's House in Malta.

A complete MST-13 timing device – a similar device was used in the bombing.

Another suspect was Al Amin Khalifa Fhimah. His job was station manager of Libyan Arab Airlines, at Luqa Airport, Malta. Police thought he had helped Al Megrahi to get the bomb onto the plane.

The **warrants** for the arrest of the two men were issued on 12th November 1991 – three years after the disaster.

FORENSIC FACTFILE

The Timing Device that Led to Al Megrahi

- A tiny piece of a **circuit board** was found in the wreckage at Lockerbie.

- It was identified as part of an 'MST-13' timing device for a bomb.

- The device had been made by a Swiss company called MEBO. MEBO had delivered MST-13 devices to members of the Libyan military in the 1980s.

- MEBO said that Al Megrahi was the man who had received the MST-13 devices. Al Megrahi even had his own personal office at MEBO.

DP/347 (a)

| 1 | 2 | 3 | 4 | 5 |
| cms | | | | |

The circuit board from an MST-13 timing device.

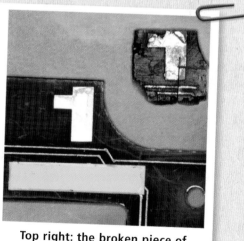

Top right: the broken piece of circuit board found in the debris of Flight 103.

The Plan

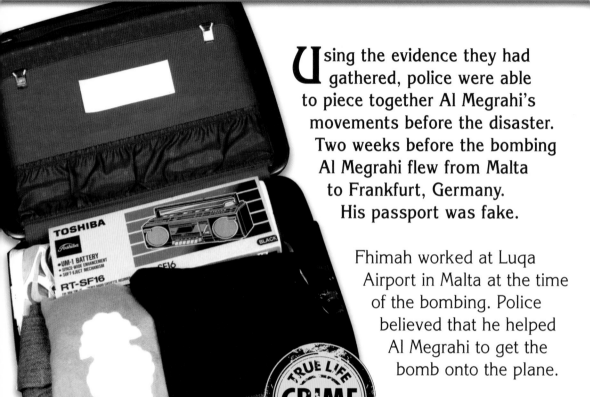

Using the evidence they had gathered, police were able to piece together Al Megrahi's movements before the disaster. Two weeks before the bombing Al Megrahi flew from Malta to Frankfurt, Germany. His passport was fake.

Fhimah worked at Luqa Airport in Malta at the time of the bombing. Police believed that he helped Al Megrahi to get the bomb onto the plane.

Forensic scientists made a reconstruction of the suitcase and its contents.

Al Megrahi hid the bomb in a cassette player, in a suitcase. When he arrived at Frankfurt, he sent the suitcase on Pan Am Flight 103 to London.

Map to show the journey of Pan Am Flight 103.

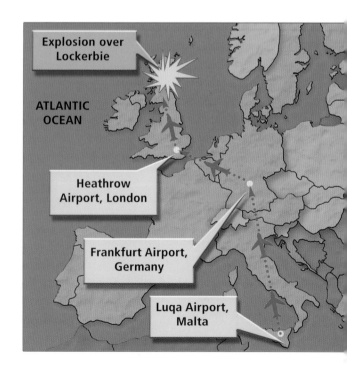

Explosion over Lockerbie

ATLANTIC OCEAN

Heathrow Airport, London

Frankfurt Airport, Germany

Luqa Airport, Malta

The suitcase had fake airline tags. These said that when it arrived at London Heathrow, it had to be transferred to Flight 103. Baggage handlers moved the suitcase onto the Pan Am flight to New York.

The bomb had been timed to explode over the Atlantic Ocean. The plan was to leave investigators little hope of finding evidence. However, the flight had a 25-minute delay. That caused the plane to explode over Lockerbie instead.

FORENSIC FACTFILE

An Early Warning?

- On 5th December 1988, a man rang the American Embassy in Finland.

- He said that a bomb would be placed on a plane within two weeks.

- The threat was taken seriously, and security was increased in airports worldwide.

- This was not true at Frankfurt Airport, though. It did not tighten security as people there did not know about the warning.

- The call is now believed to have been a badly timed prank.

Fhimah's pass for Luqa Airport, which allowed him to go anywhere in the airport.

The Trial

Though the disaster took place in 1988, it took more than 11 years to start the trial. The delay was caused by legal arguments about Abdelbaset Ali Mohmed Al Megrahi and Al Amin Khalifa Fhimah. What court should deal with these Libyan suspects? After all, many countries were involved.

On 5th April 1999, the men were taken by plane from Libya to the Netherlands. There a trial would take place under Scottish law. The trial finally began at Camp Zeist on 3rd May 2000. Al Megrahi and Fhimah were both charged with the murders of 270 people. This number included 259 people on the plane and 11 on the ground. The suspects were also charged with **conspiracy** to murder.

The Libyan police handed the suspects over to the international court in April 1999. The man on the right is Al Megrahi.

The trial lasted a year. On 31st January 2001, Al Megrahi was found guilty of murdering the victims of the Lockerbie disaster. He was sentenced to life in prison. His suspected partner, Al Amin Khalifa Fhimah, was found not guilty.

Fhimah with Libyan police officers.

FORENSIC FACTFILE

Witnesses at the Trial

The **prosecution** produced various witnesses to try to show that Al Megrahi was guilty. These included:

- MEBO employees, who said they had given Al Megrahi timing devices for bombs.

- The owner of the shop 'Mary's House' in Malta, who said Al Megrahi was the man who had bought the clothes found wrapped around the bomb.

Al Megrahi did not accept his sentence. He said that the evidence against him was false. He claimed it had been made by the US government. He made an **appeal** against his sentence in 2001, but the appeal was rejected. As of 2007, he is still locked up in Greenock Prison, near Glasgow, in Scotland.

There were five judges at the Lockerbie trial.

Case Closed

5th December, 1988

A warning was telephoned through to the American Embassy in Helsinki, Finland. The caller claimed that a bomb would be placed on a plane. Security was increased in many airports.

21st December, 1988

6.25pm Pan Am Flight 103 to New York took off from Heathrow Airport 25 minutes late.

7.03pm The plane exploded over the town of Lockerbie. All 259 people on board died. After the explosion, the plane's wreckage crashed into the streets and houses of Lockerbie. In the town, 11 people were killed.

December 1988 onwards

- An investigation began into the causes of the Lockerbie disaster. Thousands of people searched Lockerbie and the surrounding area for pieces of the plane.

- Investigators found scraps of clothing, pieces of a suitcase and fragments of a cassette player, all covered in explosive residue. Forensic analysis showed that a bomb had been been hidden inside the cassette player, and placed in the suitcase with the clothing.

- A fragment of the timing device for the bomb was found. This was traced back to a Swiss company called MEBO. MEBO said they had supplied timing devices to a Libyan man called Abdelbaset Ali Mohmed Al Megrahi.

August 1989

British detectives flew to Malta. Labels on the clothing wrapped round the bomb showed that it had been bought from Mary's House in Sliema, Malta. The owner of Mary's House identified the customer who had bought the clothes as Al Megrahi.

12th November 1991

Warrants were issued for the arrests of Abdelbaset Ali Mohmed Al Megrahi and Al Amin Khalifa Fhimah. Investigators thought that Fhimah, who had worked at Luqa airport in Malta, had helped Al Megrahi get the bomb onto the Flight 103.

3rd May, 2000

The trial of Al Megrahi and Fhimah began at Camp Zeist, a neutral court in the Netherlands.

31st January, 2001

Al Megrahi was found guilty. He was sentenced to life in prison for the murders of all 270 victims. Fhimah was found not guilty.

Forensic Search Techniques

Many different types of people are involved in searching an area for forensic evidence.

- Search teams – who look for evidence.
- Photographers – who take pictures of the evidence.
- Evidence recorders – who write down detailed information about the evidence.

There are many ways to conduct a search.

Straight line searches: The search party walk side-by-side in a straight line, looking for evidence. If something is found, the line stops while the evidence is collected, before continuing the search.

Spiral searches: The search party begins to walk in a small circle around the main crime scene, and continue to search in larger circles.

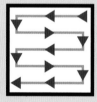

Strip searches: When a small number of people must cover a large area, they will search the area in straight lines or strips, back and forth.

Grid searches: The area to be searched is mapped and divided into small squares. Searchers then explore each grid square before moving to the next one.

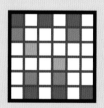

Collecting Evidence from a Bomb

Finding evidence of a bomb after it explodes is a huge task. However, evidence can be found in a number of places.

At the scene of a bomb explosion, wreckage is searched. People look for items that may have made up the bomb. These items might include:

- batteries
- wires
- **detonators**
- timers
- mobile phones
- ball bearings
- nails
- duct tape

- The injuries on victims, both dead and alive, are checked closely. Are there any explosive powders, burns or **shrapnel** in their wounds? If so, they can provide clues about the bomb.

- Every piece of wreckage is x-rayed and examined for explosive residue. Explosive residue is made up of tiny particles that are left behind after an explosion. It can provide experts with details such as the number of different explosives used, and the type of explosives. The residue can also show experts where a bomb was placed.

A mobile phone can be used to set off a bomb.

A forensic scientist checks an object for signs of explosive residue.

Air Crash Investigation

Air crash investigators try to learn everything that happened from the moment a plane took off until the moment it crashed.

- The crime scene of an air crash often covers several square kilometres. The crime scene can be on land or at sea.

- It's important to find the 'black box'. A black box records what pilots say. It also stores information from instruments in the cockpit. Recordings made just before the crash can show what happened. For example, pilots might be heard talking about problems such as engine failure.

- A plan is made of the crime scene. Major pieces of wreckage are looked at first.

- Investigators use the location of debris to find out whether the plane came apart before it hit the ground. If large pieces are far apart, this shows that the plane fell apart in the air.

- In cases like the Lockerbie disaster, the pieces of debris from the plane are put together like a jigsaw puzzle. This can show where the bomb was located.

'Black boxes' are actually orange. Their bright colour helps investigators to find them after a crash.

Glossary

air traffic controllers: Staff at airports who track the movement of planes and give pilots guidance.

appeal: Ask a higher court to change the judgement passed by a lower court.

cargo hold: The part of a plane where luggage is stored.

circuit board: A plastic card with electronic parts and wires fixed to it. These are used in machines like computers and radios.

cockpit: The room at the front of a plane, where the pilot sits.

conspiracy: A secret plan to commit a crime.

debris: The scattered parts of something which has been destroyed.

dental records: Documents made by dentists about their patients' teeth.

detonator: A device used to set off a bomb.

explosive residue: A powder made up of tiny particles from an explosion.

FBI: An American organisation that investigates crimes.

forensic: Using science in the investigation of a crime.

forensic dentist: An expert in evidence to do with teeth.

front cone: The place at the front of a plane, where it comes to a point.

fuselage: The main part of a plane, where passengers sit.

hangar: A large building used to hold planes.

manifest: A list of the passengers and crew on a ship, plane or train.

neutral: Not taking sides.

photofit: A picture of a person made by putting together photographs of different facial features.

plastic explosive: An explosive that can be easily moulded.

prime suspect: The person who is most likely to have committed a crime.

prosecution: A group of people who argue in court that someone is guilty of a crime.

radar: A system which detects the position and speed of objects such as planes.

shrapnel: Pieces of an object which has exploded.

sniffer dogs: Dogs that are trained to find drugs or bombs, using smell.

surveillance: Keeping watch over a person or place.

timing device: The part of a bomb which controls when it will explode.

unstable: Likely to change suddenly.

warrant: A legal document that allows the police to arrest someone.

wreckage: The parts of something which has been destroyed.

Index

A

air traffic control log 5
  control tower 4
  controllers 4, 5
Al Megrahi, Adbelbaset
  Ali Mohmed 20-21,
  22, 24–7
    appeal 25
    trial 21, 24–25, 27
American Embassy
  (Helsinki) 23, 26
Atlantic Ocean 5, 23

B

black box 30
Boeing 747 6, 7
bomb 14–17, 22–23,
  26, 30
  collecting evidence 29
  experts 14, 17
  warning 23, 26

C

Camp Zeist (Netherlands)
  24, 27
cassette player 14, 15,
  17, 22, 26
circuit board 21
clothing evidence 15,
  18, 19, 20, 25, 26, 27
cockpit 6, 9, 30
crime scene 30

D

debris 6, 8, 9, 10, 12, 14
dental records 12, 13

E

engines 7
evidence recorders 28
explosive residue 11, 28
explosives (see also
Semtex) 15, 17, 26

F

FBI 9, 10, 20
Fhimah, Al Amin Khalifa
  20–21, 23, 24, 25, 27

fireball 8, 9
forensic
  dentists 12, 13
  scientists 22, 29
  search techniques 28
Frankfurt Airport
  (Germany) 22, 23
fuselage 9, 16

G

Gauci, Tony 18, 19
Greenock Prison 25

H

Heathrow Airport,
  London 4, 23, 26

I

injuries 29
  facial 12, 13
investigators, air crash
  11, 12, 14, 16, 17,
  18, 23, 28, 30

J

JFK Airport
  (New York) 4

L

Libya 21
Libyan Arab Airlines 20
Lockerbie (Scotland)
  6, 7, 8–11, 12, 21, 23,
  25, 26, 30
London 7
Longtown (Cumbria) 16
Luqa Airport (Malta)
  22, 23

M

MacQuarrie,
  Captain James 7
Malta 18, 19, 22, 27
manifest 12
Mary's House (shop)
  18, 19, 20, 25, 27
MEBO 21, 25, 26

N

Netherlands 21
New York 7, 23, 26

P

Pan Am 7
photofit 18
photographers 28
Prestwick Airport
  (Scotland) 4, 5
prosecution 25

R

radar 4, 5

S

Scotland 6
Searches
  grid 28
  spiral 28
  strip 28
  straight line 10, 11, 28
searchers 28
Semtex 17
Sherwood Crescent
  (Lockerbie) 8
Sliema (Malta) 18
suitcase 14, 15, 17,
  22, 23, 26
surveillance 18

T

teeth 13
timing device 20, 21,
  25, 26
Topp, Alan 4, 5

U

umbrella 15, 19

W

witnesses 25
wreckage 6, 8, 11, 12,
  16, 19, 21, 26, 29, 30

X

x-rays 11, 13, 17, 29